rubicon
THE POETRY OF WAR

STANTON S. COERR

ISBN: 978-0-9895970-2-9

Excerpt from "How to Tell a True War Story" from *The Things They Carried* by Tim O'Brien. Copyright © 1990 by Tim O'Brien. Used by permission of Houghton Mifflin Harcourt Publishing Company. All rights reserved.

For my sons
Jackson, Collin and Tanner

May you never know the hard hand of war

If at the end of a war story you feel uplifted, then you have been made the victim of a very old and terrible lie.

Tim O'Brien
The Things They Carried

SHILOH

He walked away with only his clothes and his only shoes

And our only rifle

The men waited at the fence for him, quiet and still

Staring hard at me

As if they would never see me again

Their hats were pulled down low over their eyes so they were

> looking at me from the mouths of caves

Which was just fine cause I did not want to see their eyes and

The lying in them

They knew better than to speak to him, or to me

Or to the children

Jacob crawled along the first row of corn and wove in and out of

The stalks like the snake we saw

Last summer

Sarah stood next to me and watched her father walk away

She held very tight to my skirt

She did not cry

Shiloh

The men watched him come and I could not hear a thing
Nothing, just dead silence
No marching feet or drums or horses like I had heard
The last time

This time just nothing

These were sent for him, only for him
I knew they needed men, or that is what I heard
I wish a bird had sung or one of the dogs had howled because
This silence made it harder

I was alone now, alone before he even left, alone when they
Came
Those days ago to speak with him
Heavy voices by the fire

He had left me then, now they were here

Then quick now one sound
Abraham age seven ran from behind the house with a long stick
        against his cheek and with his one eye closed

He fired

Zippo

No quarter offered, no quarter earned
No child was spared as the villages burned
Not one man would stand up or dare show his face
As each last among us resigned from the race

Ordered and driven and scolded and thrashed
Dragged then walking then jogged and then dashed
Into the eye at the center of town
We brought the storm, and we burned it down

Out of it each man penitent came
Weeping as I called each one by his name
I held one and one went to wander alone
Nothing reversed; no way to atone

Throwing down rifles, a scream to the sky
Others trailed off down the road and passed by
Seething with anger and burning with shame
Not one of us worthy of once a proud name

Each of us little boys once, with our mothers
Then older with fathers, then older with others
Then into the tribal brotherhood passed
Grown now all at once, a real man at last

3

O B

Lopez ran down the trench and then went around a corner
            where I couldn't see him
Not a corner, really, it turned with no real authority, just a
            mound of earth that jogged left, but
He was out of my sight
So he may as well have been in another universe

I sprinted after him then the flames and roar pushed me back
Into the wall
The overpressure sucked the air from my lungs
For ten seconds I was a kid again in the dirt
After a punch to the stomach, trying to cry

I stood up and thought I was running again but was not
Down again, then to my knees
The dirt rose up and hit me in the face
I woke with dirt in my mouth and this time I did get to my feet
And started to go after Lopez

I knew he was dead: nothing
No one

Could have lived through that

Tripped over my helmet, bent, vision full of earth, put it on

Someone screamed behind me, couldn't even tell what

       language it was

Ran around the corner a second time

No Lopez

The trench came to my shoulder and I uncrouched and looked

There he was

At a dead run, alone all alone

Into the first mud hut

Who the hell knows why he was going there, we were supposed

       to wait

The strike was coming, eight or ten planes, wall-to-wall

They were telling us to get down, way the hell down

Get tight in a hole somewhere

It is not often you get a warning for the end of the world

Lopez was sprinting across open ground, miles to the door

I put out rounds, all of them, without ever knowing that my rifle

       was in my shoulder

O B

I was yelling without knowing that either

He made it and disappeared

My tracers disappeared, a snake's tail into the hut

I stopped we all did

An eternity

The black hole turned brown

He was coming toward us full speed

He was all knees and top of helmet

Carefully so very carefully cradling the baby as he returned to us

Puer

He leans forward on his elbows and spins his mug slowly
Next to but not on its coaster (beer mat....they call it a beer mat)
The water has condensed on the side of the glass, a cool coating
A very thin layer on the wood (meniscus, he remembers
At least that from high school chemistry, but not much else)

The glass floats and spins smooth above the wood
Any direction

He looks deeply into the glass, right to the bottom
Not the first to look for answers there
He will not find them because there is nothing to find
He has them already
He is young
But he is already full
He is here, right here but his eyes are away
In space but mostly in time

To the place where he is young, he is right here but seeing
Things only the old should know

EVERY NEXT DAY

On every next day, at every this time
Gentlemen, move! To the sound of the guns
Unmindful of poetry, heedless of rhyme
Move! To protect our new helpless ones

Again and again forward, and then
Pausing to listen, pausing, now hear
We move as one man, we penitent men
Enemy bigger and closer and near

The new boys among us, eyes wide, unformed
Moving along with us alone in their fear
We've told them we've been there, fighting the storm
They must not give souls to fortune's dark seer

Not far to go now, nothing yet lost
Quiet now, creeping, we older men do
Still and abashed, now fearing, now tossed
Tight as a bowstring, lads humming and new

Unbear the burden, make dear their cost
Such a good sport, this hunting of men!
Look at this red morn, this sharp morning frost
Ready to be and to give, to the end

O'er the parapets, lads, and make haste!

One last strong push for mum, for the crown

Never and no one can touch or can taste

What it means to be here! But keep your head down!

We are showing these Krauts that we'll not be ruled

We'll nae bow our heads, we'll not take a knee

We'll never stop, never, till their bloodlust has cooled

Ignore that officer, listen to me

This experience is one that cannot be bought

Will ne'er be offered, must not be sold

It is for the lads with you, this honor you sought

This race, for once, goes to the strong and the bold

So follow me, Highlanders, stay on me and run

Stay close to me, young ones, and watch what I do

Move as I do, be with me as one

I will get you home – I will see you through

Right then? We go! Over the top with you, then

Listen hear sharp, lads, and you'll not hear the guns

We go on the next day, tomorrow, again

On each of these days we unburden our sons

RUBICON

Top and bottom
Bunks like when we were boys, bodies of boys
Still boys but also
Inchoate men

For that quaternary passage
Of rites
We were first
An eclipse of each the other

Girls classes parties beer
Though always but always
Brothers

Through summer then snow and spring
Each again, and
Again, four times

Then came The
My
Our

War

Our together shrank and shrank and then

We apart and opened to nothing
Between us
Empty sad missing flowing between

He marched in ugly untidy color-splashed protest
I marched in pretty green serried rectangles
No less certain, each
To his each

He shouted hard ugly oaths against that I
Swore soaring lovely oaths
To

Our quatrain ended

The sad opening stayed though flowing and he
Threw stones in the street and

I threw
Grenades in the

Rubicon

Jungle

We marched
Each to his trumpet and
Each to the sound of his guns

Where years before we held
Stuffed bears
Asleep top and bottom
We slept now each both with a loaded gun

I traveled farther much farther and who would have thought
That
I
Only I
Would come home and
He

He would be the one who never returned
That instead he would
Die by the bullet? Instead of me?

If only the empty between had not been all between us
He may have joined me on

Rubicon

This side

Later or even then

Even if he still had crossed alone

Maybe he would

Not have

Burned

The boats

SHARK

It is in the travel that we reach our full flower

Movement itself

Drawing us out of their world and back to the one

With which we are familiar, the one in which

The internal combustion engine makes us

Dominant, not just of that place and

This time but of all places and all times

We are

Driven, driving, our machines make us whole

So it is in that momentum that we are actualized masters

Without it we are right back down on foot

With the goddamn savages

Slow, slower, stopped

We could stay here but we sure as hell aren't going to *live* here

Who could live here? Why would you?

Can't get to where we need to be

Not just slow, but slower than they, relative slow

Less used to the land

Unaccustomed to the space and the light

The time from one point to the next

So we are not just not dominant

We are inferior, weighed down with gear

Impedimenta of all of us who have been through

Renaissance and Enlightenment

Those who came out of the Dark Ages and

Became whole, if we don't have our machines

We have slid back in time and we may as well

Just fight with hands and clubs

Even then we would probably lose because we

Don't live in sand, we are concrete people with hard souls

The people tell us many of their number have never been even

    out of this village

    or over those mountains

Sidelit in sunset, shadows sharp parallel

Ridgeline and treeline barriers

While I on the other hand could speak into this radio right

    goddamn now and we would be

Standing in O'Hare

Tomorrow afternoon

In the same clothes we stand up in

We are not supplying the shooters

We are supplying the targets

If we do not move

AMERICAN DREAM

The men at the 7/11 where I go every morning in the dark
       for coffee
To stand in line with snowplow drivers and yard service guys
       and tree service guys and cabbies
Are all from Pakistan or Afghanistan
Someplace like that

They look like brothers with thick black mustaches and deep
Brown skin
They all have names with the letters all in the wrong places

Everything runs beautifully, the shelves are always full and
Taut fleshy come-hither girls beckon from the magazines
Next to a glowing ATM machine
And dense offerings behind cold glass

The coffee pots are always fresh and hot and fragrant
Because these are the sorts of guys
Who understand how important the little things
How very important
The little things

Can be

They speak to each other in a language I can't understand, Dari
      or Hindi
Maybe Pashto
Some language I can't follow because the letters are all in the
      wrong places
Their throats make noises mine cannot make
When one guy wants the other to hurry words are sharp, strong

But when they speak to me they are smiling and speak perfect
English if a little slow and have
All the time in the world
I always wonder what they were like as boys in their villages
Where there is no color at all except the
Scarves which cover the women and
No light but the sun

As they stand
Brown skin oval floating above a garish bright sea of candy
Beneath fluorescent lights
Handing tickets across the counter to those without enough
      money for this chance
To win the lottery

American Dream

One guy in particular smiles and greets me every morning
Every morning at the very same time
He moves quietly and swift, eyes down, shy
He lifts the coffee pots and wipes with great industry to keep
        the hard bright clean counter
That way

He is very delicate, thin, nearly feminine
But his strong hands are scarred
They are not calloused
Not anymore

This man walks with a limp, a bad one, one leg hurts him
He is very polite and cheerful and his eyes are down always and
I can't pronounce his name
He is healthy and young, clear eyes and skin

But he limps and
All I can hope is

I am not the one
Who shot him

IN THE RYE

Each to each
One by one
The wise ones preach and
The young ones run

No classroom blackboard chalk or text
Dare not to ask them what comes next

For better farther deeper known
Are all us uncles fathers grown
Each to each and now to I
Rich men weak men pointed, nigh

Sent upon the heath to die
Each to each and eye for eye

Sent to do
What better men won't
Better men who need not don't
The darker smaller soldier I
Am sent through the needle's eye

MALVINAS

When it was time to bring
The lads
Home from the Falkland Islands and back to theirs
They came home in two groups

The first group was put aboard the *Queen Elizabeth II* and
        steamed slowly
Taking almost a month to return to the British Isles

During that time they had long talks
Debriefs, in the parlance
What they saw
And did
They talked and drank and argued and fought
With one another

They burned the combat out of their psyches on a floating island
        populated only by those who understood and could tell
        them they were full of shit or
        that they had done nothing wrong
Sometimes both

By the time they arrived back to their island they had worked

The war

Out of their systems and were ready to return to

Peacetime service

To reunite calmly with wives and children

With the world

The second group

Got on a plane in the Falklands and was home

That day

They did not do so well

SCRIBE

Empire posting, stateless tribe
Pushed we now, but here a scribe
Will tell us hence, and hence again
Children now, adults back then

Moving, speaking and despair
Eliding now that time and there
How dare you wonder? Can you understand?
What we must do with firm hard hand?
That last one time, not known, not dreaded
We did not, you see, know we headed
Not going but sent, not rowing but swept
On one sweet brook one secret kept

They all think the snow must glisten
Because they will not, cannot listen
All who wonder will not see
Water, sunlit moon and tree
In other lands as smoothe'd stones
Washed ashore with bleached white bones

RED EARTH

I was carrying way too much ammunition as we went over the
      side
At Fort Stewart they told us that we were infantry, infantrymen
I always thought it was funny that we had "infant" in the name
For huge men carrying explosives and weapons that could knock
      down a building
I guess it means the sergeants were supposed to take care of us
      like babies, and I can tell you right now that some of the
      guys I was with cried themselves to sleep at night and
      when they talked about the farm and their mothers

When we went over the side it was every man for himself, no
      way we could help each other
I couldn't see the bottom but it was sure
Deeper than I was tall

I lost track of everyone all at once
Some of the guys who were with me I never saw again
I went under, kicked to the top
Got a breath half full of water
Went under again

Stripped the gleaming teeth, ammunition from around my neck

Dropped it forever

Took off my helmet and dropped it too

The harder I swam the quicker I sank in my echoing world so I

       kicked and thrashed

Made it to the top

Sank, and then my foot touched the bottom

Pushed

I was standing, nothing, no rifle, no helmet, just me

Naked for this world

I put my head up and emerged

A baby into the roar

TEETER

I see her now
Her arms spread wide
To hold and to be
Held

As if she knows that this day is the last
Though to the world it is not the last last

In her world it is

I see her with her arms spread wide to
Welcome in the world because
That is what she does and
Is

The way she held her arms spread wide
To be a scarecrow at
Halloweeny time

To make herself the angel in
The perfect snow

Teeter

She never wavered

Did not flinch

When it was time to hold and say goodbye

She was sad but I know that she

Only cried

Because Mommy and

I

Did

So she walked away with us but

Would not hold Mommy's hand

She walked toe to heel to toe

I watched her

Her face was away from me and her

Arms spread wide

For balance

Too Much of Nothing

Light and the absence of light in the day
Evil and hobgoblins fading away
The eeriest silence and threatening bush
Move away slowly now, minding the push
That thing that you heard in the night fading by
The sounds of the morning pulling you nigh

Clattering, shattering, rattling come
The camp starts to echo and murmur and hum
The silent dark chasm in which we were swallowed
Has opened up now as indigo hollowed
Fires and laughter, shouts, protestations
Exhausted men, darker, come in from their stations

Each man relieved from the tension of night
Ready and smiling, time now for a fight
That one that came last night fades to the marrow
In each of our bones, though sharp as an arrow
It never will leave us, not last night, not ever
Another day tarries and each is more clever

Holding a flag sharp and holding it high

Bugles and drums and stand with a sigh

Grinning now fading, feelings asunder

Cannons behind us waken with thunder

Rifles now loaded, ramrods are stowed

Each man shoulders too heavy a load

Not hot yet, not yet, but summer is coming

Each brave heart tattoos, nervous and thrumming

The quickening moment, the close call of battle

We move out and forward and grumble and rattle

Campfires out and holes all filled in

Lips to our medals to wash away sin

Nothing is soft here, nothing is kind

Nothing engages the heart or the mind

It is down to one place, first finger, right hand

The way we defend our tight little band

Hats over foreheads crisscrossing strapping

Crashing and jangling, pounding and slapping

Equipment and canteens, ammunition and rifles

No place for a photo, no room for our trifles

Nothing that you cannot eat, shoot or wear

Already this morning the thousand yard stare

Wheeling our movement, trained at the ready

Holding our line, keeping it steady

Sergeants are screaming now, officers clatter

On horses who also seem tuned to this matter

The crash roaring louder and then they appear

Other lads, other side, they are so very near

Right on the treeline there, crouching in pines

Cracks and white smoke arise from their lines

Now hoarse with the fight and flush with their orders

The sergeants yell, close us up, crisp tight our borders

Our dwindling band is a tight little square

Surrounded by others but we do not care

For others or anyone, comes now the crier

Ruffles and flourishes, orders to fire

Each man among us does what he must do

No flinching, no moving, orderly through

Each volley each packing aim cross the abyss

Each of knows he cannot miss

Perfect white smoke in one perfect square cloud

Horribly close and impossibly loud

Too Much of Nothing

We move up and now we see those in the trees

We see them, some standing, some down on their knees

Close enough this time to look in their eyes

Close enough, man enough, taking their size

Men close are falling, too farther away

Each alone in this group, on this our last day

The evil, the hobgoblins back to our field

As each man on each side refuses to yield

Closer now, too close, too many at hand

This is I know now the end of my band

The light up high strong so we see the whole fight

Comes now quickly upon us again the cold night

KAIROS

There is no way to tell how long that moment was, no way that
        he who comes later will be able
To expand it as I did
It bent just as in 1905 he said it would, curving
In and around itself
One sharp crystal point emerged and that point was me

Me alone

Compress all of yourself and all that you are into one moment of
        intensity
Sharpen and bear on who it is that you might be
For now, now it is the time for that moment, else there may be
        no other
Coiling inward and preparing is a lifetime, all that you have been
        and have thought you would be
Is here, here, right here
The moment broadens as the sun up sharp through the
Refracted haze of dark and smoke
It is dusk and dark and then warmth and light and the light is not
        always warmth, not always

Kairos

It is this day

Chronos as it always does is insistent in chopped seasoned

       increments, it is kairos of which I am here, the gathered

       instant, the perfect here now

The clarity of one-million-year-old light

The haunting great magic moves and suffuses with the new light

The last, at last, to last

Release it all that coil, release with the greatest joy into the light

Ultimate

Kairos at its work that single sharp point cracks and topples and

Again again soft in the light of the newest dawn

ZAPATA

Sergeant Cruz always threw his knife sharp stabbing into the dirt

Pulled it out, threw it, pulled it out

The sand made a pleasant sliding sound sharp in and

      smooth out

Against the titanium edge and the

Blood gutter

So it sounded like this

      schwip

      thunk

      schwip

      thunk

Right next to his filthy beautifully broken-in boot that had so

      much sand rubbed onto it

That parts of it were totally smooth

In his right one which like the left had no shoelaces but

      rather instead like all of ours a length of 550 cord which

      was really strong, the same cord they use for parachutes

 So strong a man can hang from it

He had one dog tag

Laced in and lying flat against the top of his foot

Just like all of us did in case he was shot or the vehicle exploded or he was blown apart by a bomb or artillery round

We could identify

Which pieces were once his

It was always funny to watch him get into the Humvee because

he was the size of a linebacker

Smashed into the seat, just a sheet of bare metal between him

and Macis, his knees jammed against it

He could neither escape nor attack

He didn't have any maps or a compass or really anything to tell

him where

We were going

Let alone why we were going there

Even if he had known it wouldn't have mattered because it was

dark anyway

Macis was driving and Walsh was navigating, leading his little

family, from the passenger seat

We were just following each other all in one line

In a convoy across the desert

Swept along on the current of war

All anyone

Except me

Could see was dust and the two red lights in front of him

I always felt like we should have found a smaller guy to smash

      back there

But he and Walsh worked so well together I couldn't break up

      that team which was a strong family, fire and forget

Cruz was the gentle shy giant who always had a smile on his

      dirty face and

Could have torn any of us in half with his hands but was

      the kind of guy you want to take your sister to the prom

If we got into it again

Like we did that one time

I knew he would do fine

So he jammed 230 pounds of Mexican muscle in there

Him fitting perfectly his space

Like we had heated up the vehicle and then cooled it to shrink

      tight and smooth

Around him

He always hung one elbow and the muzzle of his rifle out the

      window

Which wasn't really a window but just zipper opening in the

      plasticized cloth which

Zapata

Gave him about as much protection as it sounds like

It was 125 degrees so he would leave that door open until the
            very last second
His only acknowledgement of discomfort

The door would flash just once sharp in my headlights
As I moved around them so I could
Pretend like
I was in charge

PELELIU

Satan is here

Vulpine horror

Shredding coral, viperous dark, an evil sun

Barbed wire razors explosives bullets flame and death

Dessicated heat and blood on the rocks

Boys are crueler than men in this place, privates harder than
        veterans

All have resigned from the human race

The boys carve off ears from corpses

They are only angry about stepping through rotting human
        bodies because of the smell it leaves

On their boots

They are more casually violent than the darkest smiling drill
        instructor dream

Each man has bloody gold teeth in his breast pocket

Chilling nonchalant evil

These are the same boys who did both dishes duty and drying
        duty so their mothers could

Sit after supper

Peleliu

Who fixed tractors in the rain and bought lemonade from little

       kids down the road and

Learned to throw a curve next to the barn

Who ran to help the family on the next farm over

Bring in their crop

While the heavy storm built

Up on a black horizon

DAISY

The man's eyes were wild with pain and terrified and the snow
       white of his dishdasha was
Stained bright red, arterial blood
He had come to us because we were big and scary and armed
       and white
So we must be the men in charge
The people who would know what to do

Our doctor ran from where she was sitting in the shade as we
       laid him on a table in the
Filthy dispensary / operating room / living quarters
Where she did her work
He lay flat and still as the stain spread

She was a new doctor, sweet girl adrift in a sea
Of filthy violent men
She had the same gear as the rest of the lads, and the desert hat
       they gave her was the smallest they could find though
       still far too big, so rather than like a soldier
She looked an English lady working in her garden
We all called her Daisy

Daisy

Of all the people in the battalion not one could help him

We could kill but not heal, we could destroy but not build

Daisy was at his head, upside down to him, speaking soft female
          words in a language he did not understand

Rather than using the tools of modern medicine to combat the
          tools of modern war

She simply spoke to him

Helpless, she had never seen a gunshot before

We had come to him with violence and now he came to us

In the most vulnerable moment of his life

Daisy spoke to him, a low soothing British accent

Until he died

BRANCH

The tree has branches torn asunder
By siege, by engines, men and thunder
Deep and black, great rising roar
The generals say, "Just once more"

Leave it, lad, now...leave it broken
A talisman, a mark, a token
Example of what we can do
If put to grief, forced now to

Give it our all, stern to stem
To run right over, us through them
We the stronger, we the brave
We the right, the just, the saved

Let them see brave men and true
Start with me, and then to you

That open splintered broken branch
Tells us this side, tranche on tranche
What those above us can create
If pushed too far, by job or hate

Branch

Upon this bannock burn and clyde

Taking each man, tribe and side

One shall pair off, two together

Three or four as close as feather

Nesting now we all as one

Gone, o'er dale ere the fight is done

Gone, now in the ageless strife

Ceaseless, endless, yearning rife

With heart and blood we ever striving

Those behind calm, safe and thriving

Homeward, upward, rearward wheeling

Beseeching, bewitching...then appealing

To our one last strong great god prayers ascend

Then down to us each, one tribe to the end

Each man alone at last, each to his own

Stronger as one than each man alone

Each one among us for tribe, blood and clan

For the fight, for the kingdom, for freedom, for man

The one to my left and the one to my right

Each one alone. Together we fight

The rhythm of warriors, hard for the clan

As they deepen and broaden their knowledge of man

Each one will follow us, defending our islands

Our mothers and sisters, our village and Highlands

Shoulder to shoulder and mace, pike and shield

Locked arm in arm, ne'er tarry, not yield

Those before taught us to ignore all the bothers

Of pain, of hunger, learned from our fathers

For each of these sons we hold strong to this land

Each of them cross time, each take a stand

Each boy will follow us, one at a time

Small boy quickening, hearing his rhyme

RUSSIAN TEA ROOM

It is yesterday there

The editors right about now will be talking in fables

Like the one about the war correspondent who went native,

       who lost contact, whose stories grew less neutral

A sure sign

Of a man who has lost it, who has Taken A Side, who

       has violated the most sacred of vows of this, the most

       noble fraternity

It was not like this, you see, in The Great War, we did not

       behave this way

They will say, martinis at the elbow

We simply asked questions and filed and sent the film back in

       watertight tins

We knew our place, which was of course shown by the time –

       where was it, Fletcher, do you recall? Deauville? Maybe

       Bayeux? – Frightful time, that, it all runs together

Where we found the wine cellar? We sat with the Screaming

       Eagles officers and drank our way

Through as much of it as we could while the shells went

       both ways overhead

And my god what magnificent Bordeaux, which of course you

would expect, wouldn't you?

Being so close to the vineyards

Civilized people, and for that matter, well, yes, we must say it,

the Germans, too....cultured

The Krauts were beasts, yes of course, but their officers

understood us

We haven't heard from our boy in a while, one will say, have

you heard from yours?

They never check in anymore, do they

And when they do you can't hear a thing

Horrid telephone connections, and their copy is so bloody, so

ugly. So angry. At us, I suppose. Gone native, no

detachment, they don't understand how things are done

We can't get straight copy out of them, so after a year or so we

have to send new ones and

Bring the old ones home

They all have sunburns and their hair is too long and they have

beards and have forgotten how to dress

And they all wear those absurd bracelets

The brass ones, hammered from our own shells

The ones the tribesmen give them

GABRIELLE

Phillippe held the soldier by the arm very firmly and spoke low
Quick urgent direct into his eyes
He held his look there and did not waver
The soldier looked through him, his eyes then left, right
Down at his own soaking boots covered in mud
Then up into the hills which made a bowl with him
      at the bottom
His hand shook, just one hand, and he held a fist to try to
      stop the shaking

A machine gun rattled in the distance, to the north where they
      had breached the wire last night
Reinforcements had run through the darkness carrying crates of
      ammunition and rockets
The guns had been turned around
To beat it back

Other than the machine gun which was muffled by the heavy
      damp air
      there was no other noise
All were too spent to move

Gabrielle

No airplanes flew in the low mist

Still Philippe spoke strong and fast to the young man he held,

     their noses almost touching

The fist trembled

On the perimeter one soldier only one sang, the Marseillaise

Clear and quiet, as if to himself

DING ZUI

Filthy, cold in leaking boots
Our fate amidstream, men in suits
In warm and calm and quiet rooms
Drifting, spinning to our dooms

Peacocks tall and clipped and strong
Top hats, black coats, kith and song
So quite sure and so quite tough
Gentle some, the others gruff

But never doubtful, never wrong
Making firm and tough and strong
Decisions, only theirs to make
Ours to own, to buy, to take

Have these men not one a son
To equal reach for battles won?
Has not one man coin to spend
To push now forward, his treasure send?

To think, and twice or thrice to wonder
Darkened heart, or torn asunder?
Does he not know, that man, or see
The cold dark treasure known to me?

What now of mine here sent along
He wants, I know, that stirring song
He shan't have it, not now nor here
To calm his own soi-disant fear

Turned close to listen, near to tell
As walls and people - cities - fell
Burned and scythed and taken dear
Listen, burn, to tell, to sear

Upon the souls of quiet men
The pain and shock and then again
The next ones now, the next, the next
Not one small doubt, none too perplexed

Calm and steady, bold and strong
They seem, until they're proven wrong
Often wrong though ne'er in doubt
They send us, keep us, pull us out

Then one more time, this last, this one
Miles to go in setting sun
Down here, we are not so sure
Not one perfect, not so pure

Ding Zui

Angry protest each to each

Not carried voice beyond that reach

No man here can reason why

Or ask who'll be the next to die

RED ROCK

Come to me now and listen

Listen to what I have to say for us, to the things I learned when I

was far from you

Come and be here in the time we have made

In the space we have created, in the joy we know, in the peace

we found

I knew then that I could not be gone

I knew then that I could not be

I knew then I could not

I knew then I could

I knew then I

Would if asked do much more, more for us all

If only out from that space where it is made and it is done

Those places sent and searche'd

Long and lost, made and moded

We gather into one fierce point

Crystalline, broken

Message unspoken and from that unbroken

Tattered and taken, that which is that we center

Red Rock

Here with me, here sheltered

The whickering wind and the gentling snow

Centering steady and caviling knowns

Stasis and status, one for its other

Be with me now

Too

My son asked me if he could be like me and I told him yes, yes of
       course
When he was older and bigger he would be just like me... but
       just right then he was too young

He started to play with his toys, the small ones in the chest from
       when he was a smaller boy
I told him he was too old

He wanted to go fishing with me and asked one time and I told
       him it was too hot
The next time he asked it was too cold, and each time anyway I
       was too tired

When he asked me for the first time to go hiking with me I told
       him no - he was too small

He did not ask again

I stopped hugging him as I used to because he got too big
He wanted to go off to college and away from us but I told him it
       was too far

Too

He had the push to go to war and I told him war is too

        dangerous

Far too dangerous

He went anyway, a man

Now, though

Now I am ready for him

Though

Now it is

Too late

POINT

Shadows imagined, bushes that move
Tired minds running away in the night
Unlovable terms, manhood to prove
Throwing our longrifles into the fight

Arrows on maps and unspeakable cost
Doubling down now, into the fray
Promises broken, our labour now lost
Unanswered voices when atheists pray

One man must take us, one man must lead
One man to whom, sinning, penitents pray
One man will save us as we go to seed
One man this one time will lead us away

So forward, now moving, not nose keen to blood
Scything and churning and grinding us down
The Bozart before us now open to flood
Swirling and burbling, unseen by the crown

Onward and onward, pitching forth summoned
Pulled forward and downward, inexorable force
Thrilling once fifing and bugles and drum and
Pulled without guidance, lost on our course

Point

Always the regiment, always each lad
Keeping the faith for God, kingdom and crown
Small mothers stooped over, proud, lost and sad
Chins held up high, though, in center of town

Now, was he lost then? Eh, was he true?
Is this one now our lad, one for us all?
Tell me, did he do right by us and for you?
Did he do proud? Can we therefore stand tall?

For all of us, fighting and carrying the banner
All of us here sent boys off to the war
And all of us still there, by speech and by manner
Put all of our faith in hearth, crown and store

That young man who walks on the point, let us listen
Let us hear what he's telling us, hear what they say
On last rainy night bayonets glitter and glisten
Til one final time they are taken away

CHIMURENGA

They understand us, do they not, eh, even those

Who are not one of us? Go find the boyos

Get into the bush, mate, do it now, no use to put it off

Get, into the focking shateen where you belong

Not terra incognita anymore, brother, lekker now

All of this is ours

You will find it difficult to live there, hard to be and hard to do

      anything, any single

Thing which you find easy at home, yeh, even the little things

You'll live like a bloody animal, that's what they say, still, that is

      what I knew and

It's still the same

The things you think you can do, now you can't, right, so get

      used to it

It is so hot out there you can feel yourself going benzi,

      exploding, and you will shiver when it falls to thirty-eight

Oh and another thing, mate, listen close, now

The things you thought you knew, the reasons

Those are wrong, too

Just want you to know

Chimurenga

The focking kaffirs, yeh
Them. They are bloody savages but they are tough, tough
       as a goddamn banyan trunk, and they can run, the munts
Like a dark wind

All day and all night, so be ready for that
Oh and they can carry about twice as much as you can, so we
       gotta put twice as many boys out
Just to stay even, you see
Just to stay even

You'll nae outrun'em, or outnumber 'em, and you sure as hell
       can't outfight 'em
So you're gonna just have to outthink 'em
Listen to what the boyos tell you, do what they say, walk where
       they walk only
       listen to me: only
       where they focking walk, not a step different

Just telling you the same thing I told the last ones we sent

YANKEE STATION

The Navy and Marine attack pilots were thrown from the end of
        their ships out over the jungle in rockets with wings

You wouldn't think that it would take much energy to sit in a
        seat and move a metal stick
Two inches at a time

But day after day of this, of
Deciding whether to go above the clouds where the surface-to-
        air missiles lurked
Or down, one hundred feet and five hundred knots over the
        jungle
Where they faced a wall of bullets but missiles couldn't track

Not to mention the strain of getting back to the ship way
        offshore, maybe with
A hole in the wing leaking fuel and trying to find
A grey ship against grey water under wet grey sky
Lining up for the trap and knowing they were one hundred miles
        out to sea and low on fuel and had just this one chance
Catching a wire three inches wide at 100 knots and slamming
        the thing down

Shutting down and walking inside and debriefing and
Chow

Everyone else had just gone about their daily business on the
        ship and coming here to the officers' mess was just an
        extension of that day
For the pilots and backseaters it was stepping back into a
        different world
So they just ate and stared off
The only guy who could relate was
The guy who had been three feet away the whole time
They just looked through each other

They smiled with their mouths but that smile died halfway to
        their eyes
They both knew they would lie in bed and allow themselves to
        think about wives and children for three minutes
Then
At misty humid daybreak in the South China Sea about nine
        hours from now they were going to do it
Again

TERRA INCOGNITA

On our door are uneven marks, climbing from knee height

Snapshots

First of many rites for manly passage

You can see the progress right there, pencil on satin, scribbles:

> date and name, and if you erased the lines and stripped
>
> the paint

They would be there still, carved right into the wood

The lines are tight steady increments at first

Lowest

Then they jump, larger leaps

The story is in not the lines but the spaces

From across the room you can see how fast they were up

> and out

We knew the toughest rites would be the ones we

Could not see

Would not guide

Could not soften

The ones inflicted by others with the lessons coming not from

> adults

But from inside each boy

There would be no marks on a door, no progress to measure

Terra Incognita

Nothing to see and no sense of feel

These tests would be binary

Black-white

Pass-fail

In the sternest of schools

We fear and we know there will be no grade, just a nod

Then, a mark

These are the boys they are and those are the stern schools they

Will choose

I know this

I can see it right there on the wall

NEXT

To eat a peach
To safe the storm
A step beyond our peoples' norm
To return myself in all my pieces

Pulled to pieces
Three piece, four
Looking out, beyond your door

Thinking here and being there
Not here, not ere
Ere the long begotten stream of

Strain and strife that young men dream of
Not once never lost our nerve
To swerve
Away from you
To this, to us, to
Me and you and I were then

You knew me then but knew not how

Next

You heard the vow
I wasn't then what I am now

Me and mine pinned, under glass
Dust to dust and
Ash to ash
Not dust but earth
Beyond the sash

Told but once and forward hence
Forced to see the difference

To tell him and them and me and her
To aver

Then to part while
Close at hand
Out of reach, this foreign land

Beyond the sash a step too far
Sash to yard beyond this table
Not all I had
What I was able

REMUDA

Marching down gangways, up ramps onto ships
Casting off lines before the flag dips
Putting things right, paying debts down
Forswearing royalty, kingdom or crown

Delicate talks, then strong and bold speeches
These are things that our country teaches

These men will do it, they will take care
To put right the things we said here, way out there
These men must go. Now. They must make haste
Lest all of this effort soon go to waste

We want no evolution. Rather, speeches and swords
These are the things that our country rewards

We can talk all we like, talk of great themes
Reach into peoples' hearts for their dreams
There is so much to be done there, so much to see
For this levee en masse in the land of the free

Much less is spoken, some more to be done

Remuda

Start with all. Sort the many. Sift the few. Choose but one

Letters long lost; songs soon to be sung

Strange ancient names flow quick off of the tongue

A study of maps and a roster of forces

Cannons and infantry, guns, knives and horses

Pushing out armies to darkening lands

These are the things that our country demands

Off they go now, strong men with set jaws

Keeping the world true to this one nation's laws

Longer and faster, more sent further out

Always outnumbered but never in doubt

Quick in and out where our forefathers stayed

Telegrams. Flags. White gloves. A parade

We always succeed in these intricate dances

The greater the numbers, the greater the chances

We know the risk and we'll pay that cost

Inchoate lives wasted, recondite loves lost

For we admit to ourselves deep down in our marrow

While the road in is wide, the road out is narrow

SWEET BRIAR

The girls all laugh at me

They rib me for my nights waiting inside by the telephone

in case he calls

While they go to the dance

They make fun of my photo of him that looks at me at my desk

as I study, though I catch them studying him

So handsome posed in his blue uniform with the white collar

trying to look mean

In that photo he is strong and ready, looking off to the side like

he is looking over my shoulder, across the room, to make

sure I am safe

It seems an eternity until I will be free from here and we will be

together

Most girls are here only a year or two, like my two freshman

roommates

Both already married

I want to be off too, away from here where reading poetry

seems so silly and young

I want children and a house and I want to be with him

I know I can wait

I know I can, I have known ever since we were all at the picnic

that first summer after he graduated

Sweet Briar

Pairs had snuck off into the trees and hadn't come back

Everyone was drunk and hot

Everyone was so happy but

The weight, the time, bore on us

For we knew the boys would be leaving soon

He leaned one hand on the red-checkered tablecloth which was

       wet from the melted ice and condensation from the

       outside of all the day's beer cans

His red arms pushed against his checkered shirt

He was so much stronger than I remember he was when he was

       in college, I guess it was from all those weeks of carrying

So much weight

And running in boots and doing pushups

His hair was so short that the side of his head

Was like Daddy's face on Saturdays when I was little

Right there at the table he told me that he loved me, that he

       always had

He said to wait, to wait for him, for all of them

To come home

Sweet Briar

There were seven of them at that party, seven men

Boys, really, but men to the world

Two have already come home
To Arlington
I cried both times like I wouldn't stop
All of us cried, but it was only us girls and old people because

the boys

were all gone

So when the other girls laugh at me I don't listen to them

because I know

I have to know
That he will come back to me
Soon

ENSEIGNEMENTS

Roger Trinquier wrote the most important work ever published

        about war

About French mistake after French mistake at

Dien Bien Phu and even before that during

The First Indochina War

They looked, but did not see

They saw as Narcissus

Themselves

Rather than that which was

His book was written in French

They are the experts, the French, they have themselves done

        war well but did these poorly

It is a masterwork

Where We Went Wrong and

What We Should Have Done Better and

Why Did We Not Listen To Those Saying The Truth?

It is written for those he knew would come along

Now, long after French operations in those heavy green valleys

Were forgotten

You can find this book

Which is called *Modern Warfare*

In American bookstores

Though to find it though you must walk past the rows of

"Modern Warfare"

Video games

For the fortune of Americans it is translated into English

A very expensive book

Though not as expensive as not reading it

PASSCHENDAELE

He sits
In his chair quiet warm
Blanket and thoughts

People come to check on him
Those nice volunteer ladies
The bus goes by noisy twice each day and
There are no grandchildren

The neighborhood is still
With everyone at work and play and school and
This time of day
No one is home
But
Him

At three o'clock the neighborhood comes alive
The kids use his lawn for its perfect rectangularity and perfect
          short grass
Its dearth of trees

He leaves open the gate each morning
As if by accident

The boys are straight of back and swift of foot and full of life

He looks back through time at them

Thinks and sees them, hence, and

Hopes that the white buildings will not think up another place

      for these

Boys to go

Young men remind him of

Who once he was and will never be

It is this in which he wraps himself and that is

Why he is warm

ENGLISH CLASS

There is no way any man should be thrown like this

Being thrown, being sent, being told

The only time the passive voice apropos in war

Which is if anything active, will opposing active will

Every single thing about it, every single thing as small as what

       ammunition to carry and what to eat and when

Which pocket left or right to put things in depending on which

       side you lie on as you shoot and knowing where in your

       pack to find something in four seconds

Maybe it is the one snap that doesn't snap after six months in

       the rain

That makes the

Last

Difference

While the big decisions, the truly world-changing decisions are

       one action in a series

Decisions in which thousands of men might die and you make it

       by lifting a small telephone receiver to your ear

Pressing one rubber switch and speaking words into it and then

       those men

Go and they make decisions for those down below them and

      then in turn

Those men do the same

At every step it is a very distinct action that causes it, a verb that

      ends in –ing and makes people say much later, he did

      this and then the bad guys

Did

That

Action causes an equal and opposite reaction

Except if you are the one

The decision is being

Done

To

HARVEST MOON

Cables and fables and legends passed down
Darkness and light at the rim of this town
Something far greater, something more wise
Burns in him and moves up the light in his eyes
A boy comes a man in a place the wrong size

Small town and big dreams, carried along
Easily swayed by the siren's sweet song
The one that talks of great things and great men
The one that tells him what he could have been
The one that deep knows his heart and his ken

The only one he hears, high strong unwavered
Piercing this life, unmoved and unfavored
The song at a frequency only few hear
Him, and those with like sensitive ear
No one indifferent, but, too, none will cheer

Only they hear it, this song in each day
The one that will sweep up and take him away
The one that will bring him back home as a man
The only one that fits in with his plan
The one that he listens to, only he can

Proconsuls marching, the beat of the drums

A thrill to the heart and a deep motor hums

Braving the angry dark eyes of his mother

So men in future towns will call him a brother

Each of them, lonely, one to another

Venturing off to step into dark spaces

The gaps in his life, the filling in places

Great fortune, great strife, that constancy growing

A crystalline picture, crisp strong and knowing

One bag. A train. Goodbyes. Now the going

FATHERS AND SONS

Evanescent verities

Deep needed and hard earned

Forgotten

In the blood rush of brute primy youth

Adrenal certainty of rude male health

The howling wilderness lies before us

Opaque, frightening

Strange, immediate

A black canvas onto which we each of us

Paint our colored future

There is nothing more here

Nothing I see

Nothing I must strive to be

No one I need fear stronger than I

Onrushing reality in million-year-old light

In which we will be wiser than our fathers today

Than our grandfathers were

In which everything is good and right not just in our world, not

For those who need us but in the other worlds besides

Worlds where

Only men with guns

Can put things right

In which children

Run and laugh and caper at your knees and

Look up at you with the same big round eyes

Your own children do

And for the same reason

UPPER HOUSE

The great men read the classics in preparation for

An afternoon of governing

It is calm in that room, warm and quiet, sherry at hand

The fire pops content

Butlers glide

Proper

The playing fields of Eton lead here

None can hear that howling whickering roar

Largest sound, the one which is larger than everything

Than anything can be

That sound

Yet, again

By which we will all of us

Win

By other means

NAMESAKE

My son is six years old and he loves throwing baseballs and
        riding his bicycle and
I am his hero
He is so small in his big boy bed, taking only the top half of it and
        when I come after he has fallen asleep he is always
        sprawled across the top of his covers, and I can
        lift him and turn him and manipulate little arms and legs

Get all of him under cover
He sleeps as only
Children can

I shelter him from the ugliness of the world
From what one man can do to another because his skin is the
        wrong color
Because he has the wrong general or
Because he lives on top of my oil

My son does not yet know what can be, nor does he know what
        will be, all he knows is
What is

Namesake

His world is rounded

Fat jolly men who come down the chimney

Bunnies who hide eggs

Winged happy angels who will trade a tooth for a coin

And while

I live

He will know only this

His truth

DERECHO

Throw down your scabbard, grip tight your sword

Ignore the songs and the voices at last

Turning away now and facing up toward

All of us, each man, lashed to the mast

Notes lilting carry, diurnal birds sing

Siren songs pull us and turn slight our heads

Portent day impends, the first of the spring

Softer men, weaker men: safe in their beds

We all need your arms, your heart, mind and soul

Gather now with us, out on the moors

Comes now the time when we call out the roll

A blade sings and flashes; an arrow nocked and then soars

The gravity pull is backward not down

Longing and memories, easier times

But those men and those armies: fear, hate and renown

Will build, if we let them, the darkest of rhymes

Another sound, larger sound, builds in the marrow

Evil takes wing and the hard men return

The streets so familiar; so warm and so narrow

Pathways for watching the silent town burn

In Extremis

At the edge of survival

Each man held another

To stay warm they negotiated

Two men nested

One in front curled as in the womb

The other one leg and one arm draped

Across his partner

One man freezing on his front, the other freezing on his back

Each man shivered every moment even when asleep

Not at rest, only a suspension

In the flat opaque night and into dawn, one and the same

Close as lovers

With much more to lose

SEPULCHRE

I can see one thing, only one thing right in front of me in the
      white hot light
I cannot lift my head any farther
The soaked wool shirt of the man I march one step behind
Rivers of dirt flow down the back of his neck and disappear
      under his collar
Then reappear beneath his shirt and soak down onto his legs
They told us all that we were almost there, almost there, it was
      almost over if we gave it our all for the general, that he
      would do it at last for all of us, one last push
We had to stay with him, that is what they said, we had to
Believe in him
Like he believed in us
The same way we believe in Virginia
If we do not there will be no Virginia no more anyway

That was weeks ago or maybe months, all I know is that it was
      cold then and now the sun
Bakes through my cap and my canteen is hot on my hip all day
The dust comes up off of boots and bare feet and rises above us
      all and if a man is more than

Sepulchre

Two or three feet away from you he may as well not be there
        at all
A long time ago I could feel the rocks through the bottom of my
        shoes but not anymore
The sun is all around us every minute and
If you look up it is hazy with that dirt
It feels like someone is pricking me with thousands of needles all
        over

I think about my friend who went one time on a ship to a place
        called France which is
Far away, and he told me about the churches they have there,
        the ones that are very old
They have a high ceiling, a big ceiling way up high where you
        can't hardly even see it

You have bend your head back all the way
They have glass that is different colors
When the white sun shines it makes that glass warm up
Warm up and glow

MENTOR

Refracted wisdom

The one thing that can reverse its time

Those who came before and are more than willing than

This man

First they convince him they know best, they put their

Wishes in him, those now his, seeing what is inside as

      if it were his truly, felt not seen

A cruel prism

Each sharp sparkling unyielded expectation

Reflected wishes in hard glass

Stone, cut by flowing snowmelt

Carries along with it the expectations of man, pushes before it

The hopes of those meaner

Calm observe

Removed warmth

Forward angry confidence

Unquestioned, ad hominem

Restless and wistful

Easy, easily spoken, easily reasoned, quietly sure

This tyranny of the saved

IMPEDIMENTA

He is beneath a flag in a steel box
Packed with ice

He is at the very top of the ramp and behind him are chained
Forklifts and pallets and equipment, materiel of war
Not always interesting weapons and complex machines
Sometimes just plain old wooden crates and cranes
Crates of things and barrels of oil and
Boxes wrapped in tight clean shiny plastic

The Marines are warm marble
Hard bodies, crisp uniforms
Straight lines and smooth faces

The family is in front nearest him
Close but not close enough
Lumpy clothes, soft bodies, gentle faces

Holding each other tighter than love

The Marines are spaced out

Forty inches apart, alone, each alone

The plane is too bright on the inside, too clean, too sharp, too
        shiny
The box is which he rests is too crisp, angles too acute, too
        industrial, too perfect
For its messy ugly dirty mission

Desert brown uniforms framed against gleaming steel
Unnatural light

Marines wear gleaming white parade ground gloves with
        a desert uniform
Only for one thing

MANIFEST

Scrub pine yields sage brush, yields red rocks, yields sand
Lean horses, leathered men, here for our land

They camp in tight circles, porcupine quills
Facing outward at all of us in these our hills

The tribes fight alone, the braves each must stand
Alone, always, alone on our land

New faces, new traces, new boys in new station
The tribe and our gods, nature and nation

When he sees his sisters driven into the hills
A boy becomes man when he knows, when he kills

For all that we are and we have, we fight on
Prayers in gloaming and hatchets at dawn

APGAR

Hernandez pressed his chest into the dirt and screamed as the
      steel roared over our heads
That is what we were taught to do
To scream when a round was close, whether it was close going
      in or going out, didn't matter as far as your body was
      concerned, your eardrums would burst from the
      pressure and concussion
You would just stand there unable to receive, only to transmit
Blood running down behind the angle of your jaw
But if you screamed it equalized the pressure, or something
Sort of like when you are diving or flying
Everything has to be equal. Equal on both sides
So he did that

He screamed and I saw him with his face against the wet dirt
      mine was too
He wasn't in pain, not yet, but his face was twisted as if he was
He was doing what he had been taught
They say that when you are in fear time has a different meaning,
      that it can slow down or stop or speed up or even stretch
That is what they mean when they say everything in your life
      flashes before your eyes

Can everything you have heard flash through your ears?

I felt it in my chest and in my spine and this this this sound was

> bigger than anything ever

As large as all sound at once, compressed noise, waves packed

> tight

I know now what it will sound like when the world ends

I was a foot away from Hernandez but I could not reach him

The scream came out of him in a great shrieking whoosh from

> deep inside and I think that

He had not screamed clenched and twisted and roaring, strong

> lusty

Cry with his whole body like that before

Except for that one first time

PURPLE

The little girl in the bright purple dress runs as fast as her skinny
        brown legs will carry her
Across the desert, hard bare feet digging into sere sandy soil as
        the great large men in the great brown trucks rumble on
        the road through her village
They can see her coming, and more like her, hundreds of them
Colorful tributaries flowing from the fields and the walled brown
        compounds
Flowing gently down and then sharp up
To the road raised above the poppies
They are monster robots, hidden in Kevlar and mirrored Oakleys
        sitting behind
Bulletproof glass and armor plating
Pushing a button they can talk through a satellite

She wears half of all she owns

They are grim and exhausted, helmets down hard on their heads
Headaches from too much sun for too many days
She is not yet of her people, she is an observer of her world and
        a bystander to it

Purple

Doomed to be that way by the haggard women black behind

     black veils

The men in the truck are fathers too and they can see her, a

     purple streak against the hiding walls

Their daughters are the same size but different people

Those girls will be different than will this one, they will be parts

     of a whole

They grin through fatigue

She smiles with huge white teeth and as she runs she shouts for

     her brothers to come see and

She shrieks with joy

WAR

Relentless scything booming roar
Inside, within the chest
A deep voice shouting and a scream and less
We could and did respond with more

Every fight will sound like this
The lads they grin and put forth best
Echoing regime ancien within each breast
Knowing smiles as one first kiss

They wanted more, those callous stars
Clawing toward destiny
It seemed they wanted all from me
All from us that grasping Mars

Johnny this and Johnny that though not this time and
      not this place
It is not us but them that other race, following then
That drives us still and makes us men
As only men can track this trace

War

This time to warring running tribe

Faces painted, true words spoken

Rites of passage, not here broken

Later we will tell the scribe

Ties to the ancient race of warring men

Men alone sent forth to kill

Executing that star's will

Coming due, circling cycling then

So one by one by team by man

Not for me not fate not stars

The clear cold dark, cruelest Mars

Off to night with death at hand

NEXUS

I know that place, in black and white

A serious house in serious earth

It has been there since the dawn and was there for me and is

       there now unchanged

It is part of me and has been always

The beam is cocked above the entrance, as was mine

The walls are hardened green, sand like concrete

One side bleached

A note flutters pinned to the wood, and all I can see is the word

"Urgent" and nothing else

Is it apology, excuse, detail?

The threshold gets deeper by the day, grain by grain away

The one place where your front door changes geometry

Visitors track the threshold in with them day and night and it

       covers the maps and radios and men

Until the newest one, their own Canute, spends an hour

Throwing it all back out

The doorway gets lower, men get dirtier with their purpose

Sadder the longer they are there and there become

One at a time fewer

Of them

URUK

Kipling, Kurtz and Prufrock gone
Those we based our people on
First One, Great One, River War
Even hence the tilting score

Empire, dynasty, regime and state
Consign our youngest to each fate
If we for once will get it wrong
Will they back, e'er fore too long?

Manifested, sent by men
They will go as I did then
Off on seas and sands uncharted
Once now, finish what we started

Peoples put back in their place
By us, who else? The master race
Sent once, nay twice, to put in check
Nations strong once, run to wreck

Blood Diamond

I am not here to discover

I am not here to learn who I am

To focus wavering recondite greater truth

The clarity is not in me, but out, the

Lodestar

The greater truth I know is not the story

Not the doing

Untethered

Unknown, but not unseen

Felt

This great grand permanent ugly bargain to which we agreed is

One in which those who speak are

Ignored by those who create

Overridden by those who do

Trumped by those who would go

Ruled by those who destroy

Then forgiven

By those

Who love

ALBEDO

The bright light of the world sweeps across and shines into the
        dark corners but only for
        an instant
Nascent men sent to put things right, we wish that
Some of those places would stay dark
Once there those boys see the light, some of them

They see it and are afraid of what it holds, and they know that
        in the bright is ugly and in the dark is good
Americans fight in the night, machines and men moving in
        blackness but
Each man and that man only sees his own world

That world does not match with the world of any other man on
        either side
Technology can accelerate photons but does not turn night
        into day
It is just a different dark
The night just keeps on indifferent

No matter what each man can see, and even though each has
        his private world
They draw closer together

For the comfort that men draw from the physical presence of
      each other like puppies

Like boys do
When they are in the darkness walking home having given up
Because they can no longer see the ball

SWIRL

We must not make this happen, we must let it come

Let them come to us, let the sweep and scale take us both

When we lock it will be as whirling, circling leaves on the eddy

Driftwood in the tides

Locked together, locked with no exit, tangled and twirled in the

       last dance

One can lead and one must follow

One to move forward, one with equal grace

To fall back

The music will stop and then start once again

No point to stop, no place to rest, no moment of ease

No way out but one

YOUNGER NOW

Lighting fires in broadest light
Aching seeking then at night
He was I, I knew not how
Now, sent young into the fight

The struggle which we cannot know
Clash of muskets, sword and bow
To join the march and to the guns
Sons, dressed tight in swirling snow

Flat matte dark and forward all
Frangible, flammable, tear and spall
Churning, scything shattering shock
Rock, asunder, nations fall

Out here now, to know not when
Return in triumph if again
Front to back and side by side
Pride, that goest last in men

Younger Now

Younger now than I was then
Thrown o'er, lost in regimen
Holding fast, internal labors
Sabers, strong unto each end

He is not now nor e'er shall be
Relentless self to search and see
His piece his part his sacred vow
Now, lost, trapped but free

Give it me and here and now
Launch this for us across the bow
All us here are brothers hence
Recompense, this honored vow

Driven out beyond our shore
Same now here as studied yore
Crisp and certain, firm and true
New, asking, giving more

Men each side and chins held high
We marched as one into the eye
Beat fair, beat strong and ne'er retreat
Meet and right and, always, I

All of them and you and me

Regiment, throne and majesty

Bought and paid, by Johnny well

Each man fallen drifts alee

PAPA

We are out to sea
Rather than up the tributaries where
We began

Adrift on inchoate unreasonable yearnings for the larger
What some others call truth, though not we
Knowing

The wonder though is not this but rather whether the
Time of the genius is passed
Is this is all there is or
Shall we be again Reformed, Enlightened, renewed?

We are out
Out
Where no one can help us

JALLIYAH

Flitting, sketching, Icaran, moth
Unearne'd scraps of colored cloth
Prior battles still unfought
All that effort, all for naught
Serried grounds and praise unspoken
Bodies young and well unbroken
Offered up. A gift. A token
First in class and first in line
Master of untroubled time
Untrammeled path, his easy stroll
One alone above the whole
Too much water flows beneath
This, the sunny, gentle heath
Disguised as red in claw and teeth
Huzzahs are shouted, bells are rung
Banners high and songs well sung
Praises piled upon the other
Missives offered, one, another
One younger stood, as others ran
Impatient times, a patient man
Calm, awaits his future clan

KINGDOM COME

They lean into the wet earth, parapets towering above them
Dark walls of mud twice as high as men
Smooth faces, the bloom of the crown
Each of them has rings around his eyes, rings of filth and dirt
       and exhaustion and candleblack from the weeks
       we have been down, down

In this trench which is our country now, in eternal shadow
That is what we tell the boys, because that is what they are, all
       of them
Boys who should be at university
Not bleeding into France
The Kaiser's lads are the same, I am sure, the same young men
       broken and weeping
Gasping their last into the chemical night

We have been here so long the rounds fall right into the
       trenches with us, gunners expert now, no calculations,
       guns laid in
Ours the same

Which is why I know

If I went across for one hour I would see my boys there

Then return here to see theirs

One of ours asked me, sir, why are we here?

I said to him that this was for God to sort out but that we must

      be strong and proud for England, for the Fusilliers,

        because we above all must not embarrass the regiment

Dying is acceptable, the regiment will go on without you, but

      you must die a man

He then asked me

Is wanting to die the same thing as not wanting to live?

SOLSTICE

It's too hot for this
Too bright, burning flat glare
For this endless walking to look for things we don't want to find
For the endless talking about things we don't want to discuss
Listening to things we don't want to hear

For the endless driving towards a destiny we fear or maybe it is
        away from something of which we are afraid

We listen to neither
The people whom we are supposed to be here to help, the
        benighted ignorant lost whose fields we drive across,
        whose cows we scatter
Whose children we give candy because we can give them
        nothing else
Who want only to be left alone in their Bronze Age lethargy

Nor to our people who throw their weapons down and lie with
        their boots on with their heads on their filthy packs

Who care only about one another and don't give one good
        goddamn about

This firmament against which their stars briefly streak

Who fall asleep in the dark rooms

The rooms with

Eyebolts in the walls

The only place it is dark

FROZEN

The Civil War photographer of note was Matthew Brady

His tools even then yielded extraordinary photos

      black and white

He captured nuance and detail that today escapes even

      the best photographers, the ones who would be his

      equals now

His photographic equipment was big and bulky and heavy and it

      took time to set up and to capture a scene

During the war he had to move behind the formations

Following in trace of the huge sweeping movements, the pincers

Flanking and shuttle marches to the sea

With his big camera

Because he could not make a portrait of anything that was

      moving

All his Civil War portraits capturing its center

All of them

Are either of men who are posing quiet, leaning resting thinking

Or of men who are even more still

LAAGER

He set down his heavy machinegun in the sand with gentle love

And he coiled next to it his linked ammunition

And snapped away his harness and threw it down

And unstrapped his gear with three quick rips and let it drop
            from his shoulders

And took off his helmet and threw it upside down with a flick of
            the wrist so it faced the sky

And he lit without looking the dirty cigarette that had been
            hanging from his mouth all day

And he sat heavily on the wooden crate on its long end

And he dug two quick claw hands one into each boot and pulled
            open the speed laces

And threw the boots off

And blew a twin dragon snort of smoke through his nose

And smiled but the cigarette did not move

And without the smile ever reaching his eyes

And with the uncigaretted corner of his mouth said

"Let me tell you what I saw"

WEEK TWENTY-EIGHT

Every morning I walk to the end of the driveway for the paper in
   my bathrobe and ignore
The dog who bolts from the door as soon as the screen is
    nudged far enough for him to jam his nose
His furry body snakes through and he capers in the front
   yard
For him, you see, everything is the same. A dog has a sense of
    smell much stronger than ours, he can parse and parcel
    hundreds of smells, this I know, but could he tell when
    one was missing?

Because I could, one smell was in only one place
I could smell him still when I was folding laundry and his shirt
The one he had worn last
That still smells of both of us and comes down to my knees
    when I wear it in the house alone
I will not wash it until he comes home to wear it again, it is his
    blue shirt from college, sharp and crisp then but the
    collar is white at the fold now
The threads float from it as it pulls itself apart

It is his walking-around-the-house shirt and he put it on that day

After he had showered and shaved

He put on the cologne the girls had given him for Father's Day

The one they had picked out by themselves

Then had pedaled home on their bicycles with cards in the

       spokes and capered in the living room as they wrapped it

Deeply excited by what he would say when he opened it

He did indeed like it and he had smiled and cheered and held

       his children tightly

He was so big and they were so small

He could wrap his arms around both of them at the same time

With room to spare

MCMXVII

An ocean of space
An ocean of time
Oceans of prose, of free verse, of rhyme
Rolled out before them
Younger than now
Brought forth to battle with no telling how
Quavering, lost, but firm in their vow

Many would come back, but how many lost?
Generation unsettled, young men gone tossed

Forward and forward, and forward again
Come now, young lads, you young budding men
Come onward here with me, through to our end

No time to rest, no break from the front
Nations on nations, these men on the hunt
Chateau-Thierry, Tikrit and Cambrai
All of our childhoods taken away

Time to be men. Not tomorrow. Today

Writing each scene in his head as he went

Someday to be read by those soft boys unsent

Quiet lad stars now, a romantic tale

Our hero, of course, sized up to scale

Each firm step steady, his own reason true

But were there such men in the other trench too?

Do they not also have lifetimes to do?

Were they also center in first-person plays?

Or were they, too, cowering, counting the days?

Listening for whistles splitting the haze?

Sensitive souls with firm-clenche'd jaw

Thrown forward again and into the maw

How many of them were lost, on each dark cold day?

As their Europe sundered and splintered away

How many poems and songs, and now stories?

Long lost – forgotten – for generals' glories?

Horses and wagons and trenches and mud

Slow-moving men, creeping gases and blood

Fighting like tigers then digging like moles

Tunnelling, burrowing, down into holes

Returning to anger, to shock and to silence

Youth, joy and innocence lost to the violence

Each into himself and thoughtful and hurt

Each only two places: here, or the dirt

Always on notice, too often alert

Hardened now, fired, and stronger than steel

Night by the throat and days full of zeal

The harvest from reaping a sown commonweal

Gone now those gentle and innocent boys

After years lost with man's lethal toys

Life and those living all possible now

Emerging at last, each wondering how

Different results from the same unsaid vow

One man, to each man, king of his story

Of impossible odds and impossible glory

A Story Called Alone

We are one

Great smooth wheeling rectangle, pretty cut and glinting in the
afternoon sun from safe remove

Flashing polished steel to shiver the spine

Great Men decide

Behind battlements of breeding

Perfect decorum, clean and crisp

Safe sound and gathered round

They too in their ranks, with those whom they understand and
who understand them

Fathers, and fathers before them are

The glory of the regiment, system borne ages

As from this same regiment the battle borne, those glorious
days of story now safe told

It is to be expected, this price borne by England, the fatherland
shall bear this burden for his isles unsundered

It is the price our people must pay, simply what we must

All with stiff upper lip, all shoulder, some more than the others

Great shining moments of empire

Chosen by birth they decide

From that aerie they think we are one

58195

Who are these people
What are these, knaves?
Could they be happy as workers, as slaves?
We will show them what it is to be
People united and governed, you see
We know what is best for them, know what to do
Have seen this before, one time or now two

We ourselves did this, revolted and won
Buried the thousands, promoted just one
One man to rule for us, one who could say
That each of us men would live for that day
We will tell all of them what they should do
If they would just listen a minute or two

Put down your weapons, all of you, now
Think for a moment as we tell you how
To be more than yourselves, more like us, you see?
Is that not who you all wanted to be?
This is why we are here, the reason we came
So if you don't hear us, you are to blame

Don't talk of your people, history, land
The fact that your grandfathers fathers could stand
Strong men and good men, proud men and free
Because of their one man, the one who could see
Don't say he was one of you, one of your best
The man who united you, tribes and the rest
Don't say he's the one whom you follow now
His words the pathway, his thoughts your best vow
Do you not see us, here as we are?
Why do you look at us here, from afar?

Go back where you came, go back to your people
Your cities with pavement, your airplanes, your steeples
Your men and your women, your children, your boys
Growing up learning to play with these toys
Which you then bring to us here, set to kill
Those who believe in you, those of us still
Who know what it is to suffer your arrows
We know what you think of our stories and tarots

We savages, idiots, ignorant sons
Of those who led us, illiterate ones
Here for us all, we high and we low
We all will be stoic when we see you go

Thank you to all of you, thank for praying

To your one vicious dark god, thank you for staying

We'll follow our gods, incantations and verses

Then enlightenment happens, the spell quick disperses

INSTRUMENT

There is only one that matters truly when nation moves against

     nation

When man moves against man

It is the one who conquered the British and the Indians and the

Nazis and the rebels and

Mesopotamia

Or was it human will that did that? The will to go abroad in

     search of monsters to destroy?

A mother's willingness to send her sons

When the dark angels are loose on the world?

To go and set things right, make them our way?

Those men go, some of them, again and again

Time comes the drums fall silent

He is in the middle of thousands, alone

Soul unstirred, call unanswered

Bugles and heartstrings alike are mute in that same place for

That small boy who would not come in at dark

TQLC

The Seine in the summer flows cool and slow

The surface opaque, holding what she knows

The days when Hemingway held court across the street

Beyond the booksellers, beyond the promenade just there

With the cats (these are five-toed ones)

Sylvia and Gertrude and James and Ford

Rapt

Geniuses themselves

Ease and clarity of a bright day soothed with wine

Charged with the beautiful tension of sublime talent

That feast moved only on occasion

He had become Papa his third time there

Not the days when he sent over a bribe to the gendarmes, his

       giggling son

So he could quick strangle a pigeon to eat

That was when he was young and hungry

The Seine is aloof black majesty

Petit Pont here

Then Pont Saint-Michel and Pont Neuf echo echo twice and arch

       solid soaring dry white across

White tablecloths an amuse-bouche, dainty handkerchiefs

       framed against the Notre Dame

Floating sighing softly

In the gloaming

There are two bottles here at hand, one only begun

The other full rounded potential

Complete that second, opaque and lovely

My feet are just now drying out

I cannot feel their ache, not right now

But I will

My arms to the wrist are deep dark brick red

Then white fishbelly pale above the elbow

I am clean for the first time I can remember

I do not have the grit of that red dirt, not right now

I have a new glass

A new round clear glass for each new full pour

Crisp clear crystal clean

Then opaque and still and deep red dark

TQLC

I read in college that you can tell the quality of a wine by looking

At the top, at the very top, and if you tilt the glass just a bit

there will be a clear layer

Holding tight strong clarity above the complex depths

A good wine will give herself up to you

You will know it, just know

Like love, or fear

You know

There is no yesterday and no tomorrow

There is only right now

I know that

Papa had the words for it when he sat quiet, right here

Young and hungry from his war

STREET

Just the same here as it is there, same poor helpless people
Same big dudes with guns

We own that place, yeah, and we own this one too. Well, maybe
  there is a difference. Tell you what it is. The difference is
  that there everyone is scared of us and don't do nothin
  'less we say
They know good and goddamn well that if they open their
  mouths that gonna be it
Shitstorm gonna come down on 'em and ain't nothing we can do
  to stop it
Cause they know and we know, one word to one chuck cop and
  that's it, cops all over the place, it'll take us weeks to put
  it all back together, and that's a lot of money right there

Ever since that thing two summers ago ain't nobody say a word
  to the cops, and when something do happen, nobody
  can remember nothin, and that's the way we want it

Nobody remembers. Ain't nobody gonna remember

The people here are scared of us too, but they don't run inside
      or hide or nothin when we come. They just sit in that
      weird way they have, down on their heels, they can sit
      like that for hours. They just stare at us
They hate us, we know that, but when they look at us it's like
      they starin' a thousand miles
Like you could shoot someone right there on the road and they
      wouldn't blink

They tell us grunts that we have thousand-yard stares but we
      ain't nothin compared to how these people can look
      right through you
Maybe it's because they seen a lot more than we have. Maybe
      they got nowhere else to go
Oh, and there's one more difference: we got better weapons
      over here. Way better
I 'm gonna remember them stares when I get back on the street
The real street, I mean.
The other one. The one where we win

DIGNIFIED TRANSFER

Remains

What does that mean?
More of him
Remains

Than what is beneath the flag

www.ingramcontent.com/pod-product-compliance
Lightning Source LLC
Chambersburg PA
CBHW070635030426
42337CB00020B/4026